D1324203

THIS IS A CARLTON BOOK

The Dog Logo and Photographs © 2005
Artlist International Inc
Text and Design copyright © 2004
Carlton Books Limited

This edition published in 2005 by
Carlton Books Ltd
A Division of the Carlton Publishing Group
20 Mortimer Street
London
W1T 3JW

A CIP catalogue for this book is available
from the British Library.

ISBN 1 84442 694 7

Project Editor: Amie McKee
Art Director: Clare Baggaley
Design: Stuart Smith
Production: Caroline Alberti

Printed and bound in Singapore

THE DOG

Artlist Collection

CUTE **PUPPIES**

CARLTON
BOOKS

American Cocker Spaniel

American Cocker Spaniel

Shetland Sheepdog

Shetland Sheepdog

Border Collie

German Shepherd

Bouvier des Flandres

Doberman

Akita

Akita

Akita

Rottweiler

Pug

Old English Sheepdog

Boston Terrier

Newfoundland

Poodle

Flat-Coated Retriever

English Cocker Spaniel

Golden Retriever

Golden Retriever

Shih-Tzu

Bernese Mountain Dog

Chihuahua

Irish Setter

Dalmatian

Bichon Frise

Saint Bernard

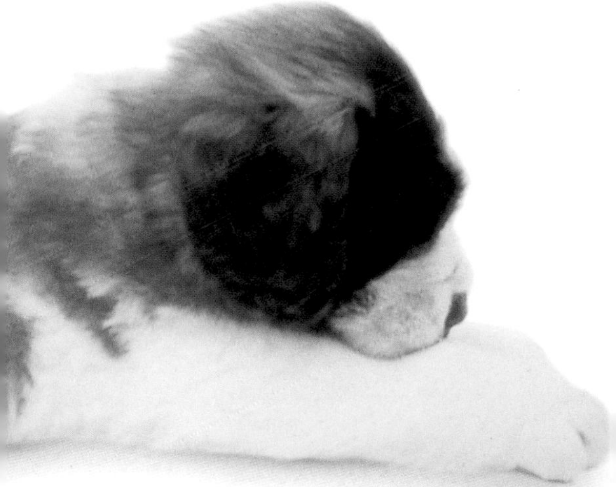

Saint Bernard

Dachshund

Miniature Schnauzer

French Bulldog

French Bulldog

Pembroke Welsh Corgi